TELLING YOUR STORY:

How to Reinvent Your Web Presence and Attract New Customers

By

MARK ORION

This book is dedicated to all of my clients who have created enduring stories that have enriched readers all over the world.

Their websites are a living testimonial to the power of story in building Internet communities.

CONTENTS

TELLING YOUR STORY:

HOW TO REINVENT YOUR WEB PRESENCE AND ATTRACT NEW CUSTOMERS

CHAPTER 1

Is This Book For You?

I fix websites. People call me when their website is failing.

This book is about using the power of story to reinvent your website. The principles in this book can make all the difference between success and failure for your business.

Let me start at the beginning. I've been very fortunate to work with some of the finest Fortune 500 companies as a web producer and web strategist.

I have directly facilitated and managed the ongoing development of business websites since the early days of the Internet.

We've seen some amazing growth in communications and how business conducts their day-to-day operations as they interact with customers.

Is this book for you? Well, here's some of the questions that you may want to ask yourself.

Is your website outdated? When you look at your revenue stream, is your website significantly contributing to your bottom line? Do you feel like your competitors are ahead of you? Do you visit their websites and find your own website lacking?

Now let's ask a few more questions that really zero in on a few key issues. Here's a great question to ask yourself; has it been three or more years since you've updated the content on your website? Let's expand that principle a little more.

You would be surprised how many businesses never refine their marketing message that is displayed on their website. There's been no iterative learning. They still think about their website the way they did eight years ago. And that just doesn't cut it in today's marketplace.

Content is King

This book is about fixing your web presence. About creating new Internet content that speaks the story of your business.

Content is King. Now more than ever. If there is any singular message to this book, that's it.

When I'm called as a consultant I often see

patterns. A very common scenario is the inability for objectivity regarding the primary company marketing message transmitted over the web.

I know that's a mouthful but it true. Sometimes the business is so immersed in their day-to-day operations that they have a difficult time examining their marketing with a fresh perspective. They can't see the forest from the trees. They are blind to the simple story their customers perceive.

That's what this book is about. The actual story that you're telling.

There have been a number of studies that prove conclusively that the marketing story you share with your customers is what they remember most about you.

Plus, as any savvy Internet marketer will tell you, the most effective advertising is word of mouth. When you tell a compelling story, you give your customers something to tell their friends.

Again, that's what this book is about.

This book is for you if you need to jumpstart your business.

This book is for you if you've lost a feeling of excitement and passion for your business. Telling a new story can bring the life back into your products or services.

Build for Your Future Success

This book is also for you if you're interested in building a future as the Internet continues to expand. The most powerful currency is mind share. Telling your story builds mind share.

This book is for you if you wish to enhance your ranking in the search engines.

Later on in this study we'll talk about the absolute fairness of Google's organic search listings. I'm talking about the non paid listings. Time and time again, a business owner will ask me how they can increase their rankings in Google.

This book shares that solution. We share with you that, in fact, there is no magic shortcut. To rank high in Google, you must earn it. And the way it's earned is to provide worthwhile content to your specific niche audience. So read no further if that's all you wanted out of this book.

But by all means, please continue reading if you'd like some ideas on how to achieve that.

Nothing Stands Still

Technology keeps changing. It's not gonna stop.

I've been in the business since the web began. I've watched the changing technologies and participated through the various phases of web evolution. Now, granted, there certainly are times when we advise technological changes required for a client's web presence. But that is secondary to telling the correct story. Story must always come first.

As I stated before, content is king. The future of your business is dependent on the quality of your content.

Most websites fall short in delivering a clear story. People remember your story and that becomes your identity.

Never forget, as far as your customers are concerned, perception = reality.

Change your story and change your results. Simple.

So here we are. Many people need to reinvent their websites. The thing that most needs to be reinvented is the scope, purpose, and clarity of their story.

Once your story is clear, redesigning your website becomes very easy.

All good? Great. Let's get started!

CHAPTER 2

Crafting Your Story

We're going to talk about a number of different ways to craft your story. Therefore, we're going to speak about principles.

For the sake of this book, I'm going to define a principle as an overriding idea applicable to any specific variation or situation. No matter what your business or service these principles will work.

I would suggest that you not try and write your story until considering and examining all of the principles in this book. The principles are designed to assist you in specifically identifying, crafting, and subsequently telling your unique story.

Identify Your Strengths

So let's begin with a very useful principle; lead with your strengths.

What you do better than others? What are the

best areas of expertise?

What is it about your story that highlights your unique accomplishments?

Everyone has areas of expertise. We want to identify yours.

Shining a Spotlight

We want to shine a spotlight on your strengths. We went to zero in on the things that you know about your business that no one else does. True, there might be other people involved in the same type of business but... they undoubtably don't have your unique fingerprints.

By finding your strengths, we illuminate the areas that will make your story compelling. We want to highlight strong points that you probably take for granted. Skills that others would find amazing. That is, if we include them in your story!

Knowledge is power. The Internet rewards expertise. So does the marketplace. We all love to talk to somebody who knows a topic or market better than anyone else. We want to make sure your customers know you are an expert.

For example, whenever I learn a new skill, one of the things that I look for is someone who can help me focus on the truly important and relevant topics to learn.

For instance, let's say I am exploring learning software associated with the new skill. There are usually so many different brands and types of specialized software out there that just knowing which one is worth putting my time into helps a lot. For example, if you're interested in learning graphics, time spent learning Adobe Photoshop is time well spent. You get the idea.

Whatever your strengths are, we want to lead with these areas as we craft your story. Simple.

Again, we want to share your expertise. Expert stories are constantly in demand. Plus, you expand your market when you're asked to become a guest editorial blogger or to assist someone as they tell their story. More on that later.

A Fresh Perspective

Many times it's very valuable to bring someone in from the outside. They can look at your strengths in a new light. Never forget, many of us take our expertise for granted. Especially in specialized areas that come easy to us. For others it may not be that easy. All the more reason why it's important to have a fresh perspective from the outside.

As you examine the strengths that you possess, break them apart into groups.

Let's say you're an expert on motorcycles. Now,

let's break it down into different areas. You can tell a story about how to select a frame. Another key area could be in rebuilding an engine. Each of these areas can be expanded as you tell your story. Each area will appeal to a niche audience needing your expertise.

Perhaps your strengths might be in an area such as bringing people together. Creating conversations is a very empowering aspect of Internet communications. If it is one of your strengths, we want to make sure we include it in your story.

Selecting How To Tell Your Story

Another reason why it's so important to find your strengths is to assist in selecting what platform or tool is best for the actual delivery of your story.

Is Internet video the best way to communicate your information? For some stories, it is the most effective. A blog? Perhaps free weekly seminars at a community college?

As you locate and identify a specific thematic element that tells your story effectively, you'll be led to the best platform to share that communication. For instance, if your strength is visual communications, video may be the most effective route for your message

Always keep in mind, it's usually a good clue if something comes easy to you. That's usually associated with something that is a strong area of your skills. What comes easy to you... might in fact, be very difficult for your customers.

Get To The Point Quickly

We want to find your strengths and lead with them. Telling an effective story and reinventing your Internet marketing is going to hinge on your ability to reach people quickly.

Getting right to the point happens easily because you know your story. You want to cut through all the stuff and get to the point. Lead with your strong material first.

Writing a blog post? Telling your story means leading with your strongest material at the beginning of any article.

By knowing your strengths you can position your article correctly. You want to lead with the most important content first. If you don't lead with the powerful stuff, folks are going to leave before they get to it.

Never try and slowly build to a point when you're writing for the Internet.

As an example, if we're making an Internet video, state the most important points in the video first. Let's get to the story punchline ASAP. Then we can go into the details that supports your story.

The days of leading up to point at the end of the article are over.

Defining Power Positions

A power position is something you do better than others. That's what will give you expert credibility on the Internet. How's that for brief and to the point!

Educate, Not Try and Convince

That's the difference between effective Internet communications and the old school of writing. We're not trying to convince people. Were trying to educate them. There's a big difference.

When you're actually saying something of value, people appreciate you getting to the point. (Hopefully, I just did that!)

In fact, in the Internet age, we hate people who waste time.

Come in the office. Give me the information. Now, please, um... get out. Familiar? That's the mantra nowadays.

Only One Position Per Article

This one is key. When you tell your story have one objective. That's all you need. One idea.

When you take one position and keep reinforcing that one position, you achieve several benefits at the same time. Not only do you increase your odds that people can hear what you're saying, you also increase the odds that metadata is going to be consistent for the article. That's part of the new way of telling your story. Metadata has to be indexed or search engines will not return appropriate results during searches by your customers.

And the way that is achieved? Consistency. Clarity and singleness of your story. Now we're cooking!

As I stated earlier, say your most important thing first. And just one position.

Our goal is for you to own that position in your customer's mind. The power of positioning.

Tell the same story over and over but do it in different ways.

Repetition works. It also helps you to be found by different customers who come from different search engines since different search engines use different algorithms to collate data and subsequently return search results.

If You're Too Shy On Camera, Stay Off Camera

It goes without saying, as we define your strengths, we also acknowledge your weaknesses.

If you're not good in front of a camera, don't be out there on YouTube.

Get someone else to be your spokesperson (if that's the medium that you want to tell your story in). We went to keep your story strong. So do what you do best. And stick to that. Your customers will appreciate it.

Trust Your Intuition

Your intuition is your friend. It usually points to your strengths. Listen to yourself.

Your intuition will help you identify your strengths. Pay attention to the aspects of your business that comes easiest to you. There's an interesting principle that occurs as we tell our story. The things that we find interesting, well... others will too.

Never Be Boring

That's a very important law of storytelling. If it's boring to you it will be boring to others. Never bore your customers.

If you have to shock them to keep them awake, do it.

Ideally, don't let yourself become boring, because in this Internet age, people will be gone at the speed of light.

People will fly off your website faster than you can say "negative page rank".

CHAPTER 3

Narrow Your Focus

Next, I'd like to talk about how important it is to narrow your focus.

The era of overgeneralization has ended. One of the things that I run into often with clients is their failure to identify a specific niche market to serve as the target for their marketing story.

Your story should speak directly to the customers you want to attract.

Craft your story for a specific audience. Start fresh. A new approach to reach your select customers.

Solve Their Problems

When you craft your story, you have to always be narrowing your focus down to appeal to the mindset of your customer. What are their real concerns? How do you solve their problem(s) for them?

Narrow Focus Is Easier To Port To Diverse Platforms

Another benefit of narrowing your focus is that it makes it easier to carry that same message across diverse platforms.

Different platforms require diverse methodologies in sharing your story.

Whether we're blogging, making a video, or using any other method of communication, different diverse mediums will require refining your message to effectively reach your customer base.

The ability to send the same story regardless of the medium keeps the story consistent. Regardless of how the story is transmitted.

And... a narrow focus helps us stay on point regarding your objectives.

Identify Profit Centers

As you reinvent your story, examine your revenue streams. What aspects of your business really bring in the most revenue? Follow the money. What products and services of your company help people the most?

Use the power of a niche focus to tell a story

that supports your profit centers.

List the three profit centers that contribute the most to your business or service. It's usually a good idea to start there.

How can we focus on those areas and craft our story based on reaching our customers who could most benefit from what we offer?

With access to worldwide markets, unlimited opportunities are available when we narrow our focus.

Narrow Focus Helps Positioning

The more we can narrow our focus, the more we have an opportunity to achieve a number one position in the customers mind. Tell the story about what you are most passionate about and be the best at it. That's a winning recipe no matter how you look at it.

When we narrow our focus we also immerse ourselves in the specific problems that we're trying to solve. We're speaking directly to our customer concerns.

We all know what it's like to go out and search for information and how great it is to find an answer as quick as possible. That's the power of narrowing your focus.

By reinventing our approach we open our

minds to taking a new way of looking at things.

Another reason to narrow your focus is it allows you to craft your story around areas that you actually enjoy the most. Irregardless of the scope of any business, there's going to be certain things you like most about your business. Therefore, it makes most sense to accentuate these areas.

Spend time telling the story that you want to live in. Plus, again… the odds are better that you will reach your target market.

So let's recap. Narrowing your focus lets you define your customers. It also allows you to organize metadata and other technical aspects which are going to make your data easier to find.

Remember the power is in the niche. You want to be regarded as the expert in your key areas.

CHAPTER 4

Create Conversations

Many times when I start working with a client, one of the first things I ask is what are they doing to encourage and create primary marketing conversations with their customers.

It's very effective in building our organization when our customers talk about our products and services amongst themselves. Especially if it's favorable information concerning our story.

One of my clients is involved in the hair design industry. As we sat down to create her story, it became very clear that her niche would be enhanced by setting up a platform for all of her clients to communicate. The opportunity involved creating the appropriate communications structure for her customers to freely share their tips and tricks about her product lines.

Following the creation of online product forums, her clients now post and blog about best practices for using her products. As they discuss her products, she also participates by providing her ongoing consulting and expertise. She also tests new markets and previews ideas for additional products. As she has said, feedback from her customers continuously helps her to refine her products and services.

All of those benefits are derived from simply facilitating and creating customer opportunities for conversations.

With all the different tools on the Internet such as forums, blogging platforms etc, there are many possibilities.

There's never been a better time for creating conversation among your customers.

CHAPTER 5

Facebook and Social Media

Nowadays everybody has a Facebook page. You might be surprised to see how many companies pay no attention to the marketing message that goes out on their Facebook page.

For successful modern Internet marketing, it is absolutely imperative that you maintain focus to ensure that your Facebook message stays congruent with company objectives.

Ideally, the same editorial web team that designs all of your content is also handling every bit of your social media. This extends across the board to all of your social media.

Because of the diversification of the different types of social messaging, it's very important that anyone who administers your story understand the differences in all the platforms they're releasing content on.

As an example, effective messaging on Twitter is completely different than creating content for Facebook. It's very important that the message is clear. When your marketing story is clearly defined, it becomes easier for you to create variations of your story where all the variations maintain the same theme. Consistency is key. Irregardless of the platform.

And again we can see the importance of the singular powerful position. A simple position that occupies your customers mind. A marketing story that can be extended across any social media.

When we carry this story and extend it to every kind of social media platform we can then experience the positive benefits of diversification.

CHAPTER 6

Offer Your Services As a Guest

As a subject matter expert, you can contribute to others. One of the most useful ways we recommend clients share their story is to offer their services to assist others. This can be accomplished via appearing as a guest on blogging platforms, online video shows, podcasts, or any other way that you can share your information.

As a recognized expert in your field, your opinion matters. By appearing as a guest you gain credibility. Plus, this also provides many opportunities to reach new audiences.

I worked with one client who contacted a local community college and every Wednesday night for two months gave a free hour-long seminar.

The first three or four times no one showed up. They held to their plan and eventually the word got out. Now they're providing these same seminars on a weekly basis to standing room crowds. The local paper also did a feature on them which brought more people to the seminars.

As they shared, their new story has also made a positive difference in other areas of their business. After reinventing their business to include free seminars the word of mouth has spread and they are busier than before.

As an interesting side note, due to their increased profile in the market place, they've actually been able to raise their prices. They're giving more and in turn their services are in greater demand.

Chapter 7

Your Perspective Matters

As an expert in your field, your unique point of view is very important. It forms the bedrock basis for your expertise. Your perspective matters because your expertise communicates trust.

As you reinvent your business, you are uniquely qualified to tell a story that you know is accurate. As an expert in your field, your surety benefits your customers.

To thine own self be true is a powerful guiding principle. To the degree that you develop this philosophy, you will increasingly be respected and acknowledged as an expert in your field.

That's a positive story you want to be bringing to your customers.

There's another reason for us to discuss these principles. One of the things I enjoy most is helping my clients end their ambiguity. Working with a wide variety of businesses, I've often observed companies that are always second-guessing themselves. It's like they're chasing some imaginary goal outside of themselves.

Any time they perceive a shift in the external market they put themselves in the position of reacting. Please note a very important distinction here. You will remain lost as long as you base your company on reacting to marketplace fluctuations. You must base your decisions on your own choices. Choices with a foundation in your story.

Take a stand. Become someone who leads by action instead of waiting to react.

Therefore, your perspective matters. Ask yourself honestly. How might you genuinely help people more? What are the weak points in your industry? Where does your product or service fall short and fail to meet customer expectations?

Because your perspective matters, now is the time to address all of this. Right now while you're crafting a new marketing story. Reinventing your business using your best instincts rarely disappoints you. I've seen this over and over as I consult with companies.

I would love it if people read this book and put together marketing stories that place their company in a better position than they've ever been before. Where they enhance their products and services and become the best.

Irregardless of your business or service, we want your customers to be coming to you because they feel you're the best. That is achieved via your story.

Your perspective does matter. You know what works in your given field. With years of experience, you have a lot that you can bring to the table.

That's what your customers want from you. They seek your experience that will help them solve their problem(s). You can't become a problem solver without the loyalty, convictions, and belief in your own solutions. Without that kind of surety, there's no reason for a customer to take a chance and trust you.

CHAPTER 8

Stand for Something

As we continue our discussion regarding the power of your story, it's important that we address what you stand for. Ever since we were children, stories always had a moral to them.

The best stories have a moral. The same holds true for your business and service.

Even if the moral in your story is change your oil more often to protect your engine, it's still a moral of the story.

No matter your product or service, we want to make sure that you stand for something. We want you to base your story around something that is meaningful to you. No one can tell you the specifics. You have to arrive at that yourself. We can, however, suggest your company take a position based on your story and stand for something.

Everyone understands that. It's your choice. First, decide what is important to you and then stand for that.

Have Your Act Together

When we have our act together and communicate our beliefs to customers, it becomes simple to tell our story. The story will always come out the same way. It'll support our marketing initiatives plus make it easier for us to occupy a position in our customers minds.

Let's use an example of a craft store. Now, someone might think there's no real story or belief system involved in a craft store. That's not true at all. I can think of one store that is consistent in telling their story in everything they do.

First of all, the store is run by two women who put everything on the line to go into business. They are committed and have a stake in the game. What's more, you matter. When you visit their store they personally engage you in conversation. You get a chance to actually get to know them. Because the store is in a small town, they are regarded as an important part of the community. Their customers understand and support their story.

Their story is based on handcrafted quality. They only bring items into their shop that have been made by local artists. The only items you'll find for sale are priced as one-of-a-kind items. That's part of their story. You don't go there looking for a bargain. You go there looking for a one-of-a-kind artistic piece that supports their story. Their story supports the local artists. Anyone who purchases items at the store doesn't mind spending the extra amount because they know it's for a good cause and they know they're getting top quality.

Their story is consistent with everything. The location of the business, the cleanliness and care that goes into setting out each item for sale, as well as the monthly craft shows where they bring in the artists to show their goods personally. Everything backs up the lifestyle.

Their story is based on their ideology and their support of fine craftsmanship. They stand for something. As a result, and not surprisingly, their Internet business has taken off. People from all around the world purchase goods from their website because of the market position as told by their story.

They stand for the kind of commerce that many have said no longer exists. It's true, they don't get the customers who might be going to Walmart. They do however, get the customers where money is no object. And that is consistent with their story.

CHAPTER 9

Your Unique Value Proposition

What is it that you do that no one else can provide? That may or may not be the case. If it is, you are highly blessed and very fortunate.

Jerry Garcia of the Grateful Dead once stated that the Grateful Dead were the only ones who were doing the exact thing they were doing. He was making a great point. He stated "You want to be the only one doing your thing". Now in this era of differentiation this principle takes on even more importance.

Define It and Own It

When we reinvent your business we want to tell your story so we define your unique value proposition precisely.

We want to make it clear that you are the expert in your field. No one else can do what you bring to the table. You can see how the principles we've mentioned this far in the book all contribute to this position.

Even if there's a lot of people doing the same kind of thing you're doing, we need to isolate and illuminate the precise difference in your product or service.

You can see why it becomes so important to have that unique position and perspective. As a consultant, I often see things the client has overlooked. I often see their strong points immediately. I see that they're the only ones offering their unique value proposition.

Once I spot their unique value proposition, I waste no time in pointing it out. That's the kind of thing that sets the entire campaign in a new light. A unique value proposition is your ticket to high search engine ranking.

More About Search Engines

We've mentioned search engines several times so far in the book. That's a worthwhile use of our time and I don't mind talking about it some more.

When we tell your story correctly, ideally, your unique value proposition becomes clear. Now, if we're creating content correctly (a separate art in itself), the search engine algorithms are going to be able to pick this up. When a customer does a search on Google they're going to find your website.

Again, how we make that happen is through a variety of different methods. It's not within the scope of this book to go into a lot of the technical aspects that go into creating tags, titles, and other specific disciplines of creating Internet content. Suffice it to say, that there are professional ways of creating your content. When these ways are followed, you in a position where Google can index you website based on a fair evaluation and assessment of your business.

That's why earlier when I spoke about Google, I spoke about fairness.

So far, and hopefully it'll stay this way in the future, a positive page rank can be achieved when you fairly provide value to your customers.

As I mentioned, this is best achieved by a niche appeal that is very specific. That's the best way to show up on search. Be highly specialized and have a lot of content that supports your clear and unique market position.

Revisiting Metadata

It's worth it again to call attention to the modern importance of metadata. Past generations didn't have to think about tagging, data analysis, and the overall global understandings of metadata required for appropriate product positioning.

In other words, it's one thing to be able to state your message in your story, it is equally as important to understand how your data must support your position so people find you.

Metadata is an important part of your Internet strategy. Metadata as we discussed it before is information that is about your information. That's a pretty simple way to put it but for our purposes gets us into the ballpark.

Let's consider another reason why it's so important to have the same minds sculpting your entire strategy. It allows them to think ahead and create a metadata roadmap. When we know what story we want told for your company, we can at that same time create our overall strategy for tagging and metadata. That can make a big difference towards the effectiveness of your Internet campaign.

And to pitch this again, always look to specialize. Avoid being a generalist.

For a dog grooming service, as an example, you're much better off if you're the very best at doing small dogs. As opposed to somebody who says we do all breeds. When you specialize its easier to tell a story that can be found by your potential customers.

Google will index you better if you're specific.

So, for instance, if somebody does a Google search for small dogs grooming, guess who shows up. Not your neighbor who markets from the position of we do all breeds. All breeds is not going to trigger the same search algorithms as the company that specifically is talking about small breeds.

So are people getting wise to the power of metadata? Are they learning that it's important to specialize?

Fortunately, yes. This is getting better. More people are starting to understand this. In the early days of the Internet it was a real problem trying to explain these principles to somebody used to generalizing everything. So many businesses wanted to fly out the entire menu of all their services. It just created confusion.

Here's another example.

Jack Of All Trades Is Not Effective Anymore

There's been a few times when I've been called upon to assist companies that provide handyman or general construction services. Their problem is hanging out too many shingles.

They try and be too many things at once and the end result is they appear like they're not an expert in anything. That's often the dilemma with many services and occupations.

You're much better off to do one thing and do it well.

Do it better than anybody else and base your unique value proposition off the surety that you're the very best.

Your unique value proposition also puts you in the position of receiving positive word of mouth. All of us have friends who sometimes need the same services and products.

I'm sure we all can think of examples when somebody has asked us for a referral. If your unique value proposition is solid and you're telling a story that correctly highlights your strengths, you've put yourself in a great position to be recommended.

And that's the best method of securing new business.

CHAPTER *10*

You Must Know Your Motivation for Your Story

As we go about reinventing your web presence we have to examine motivations.

In this era of Internet savvy consumers, it's to a company's own peril to ignore the sophisticated nature of their customers. People have been pitched so many products that they can smell a con from a mile away. That's putting it pretty bluntly.

As you go about sculpting your story, your motivations will be picked up by your customers. That's one reason why we've been speaking so much about integrity in this book. Your reputation on the Internet is worth all the money in the world. Reputation is everything.

Here's a classic example of true motivations being quickly understood by customers. One of the most ridiculous practices is where a business sends you a so called birthday email. Ridiculous and shallow, indeed! I even got a happy birthday card from defensive driving! That'll teach me not to get a speeding ticket! Any thinking person understands their motivation is to use your birthday as an weak opportunity to pitch whatever they're selling. That's the type of insincere marketing that loses customers. The kind of lame efforts that actually hurts a business image.

Therefore, it's so important that your motivation is to honestly help people. Ideally, your product or service makes people's lives better. That's a worthwhile endeavor and people will sense that.

We all endure thousands of advertising messages every day. Some are not very subtle, some are very subtle indeed.

Either way, like it or not, we're being pitched all the time. Your motivation will set the tone as we tell our story.

If we focus on helping people, our audience will sense this. When you reinvent your business you have a prime opportunity. You can choose to do something different. Let's examine a few reasons why you may want to.

As a consultant, I'm often called to speak to a business. Now… when do they call? You got it.

When they're in economic trouble. That's often when they call in the consultant.

After all, tough time create a willingness to call for professional help. I can't tell you how many times I find people who have not spent any time examining what attitudes and behaviors created the situation. If their business is in bad shape, what did they do that created those bad conditions?

It only stands to reason that if we keep doing what got us into economic trouble, the very nature of our problems will continue to escalate.

A bad story will perpetuate itself. Unsuccessful methods and bad marketing stories need to be changed ASAP.

Focus On Helping People

The smart business person realizes that when they focus on helping people they benefit in many ways. To begin with, at the end of the day they feel good about themselves. That alone is enough reason to do this.

But there's many more reasons why telling your story in the light of genuinely helping people makes good sense.

As I mentioned before, we are all discriminating consumers. Even children can quickly sense the motivation in communications. In fact, sometimes they're better at it than adults.

As we focus on reinventing your business, it's

important that we tell the story that will make another's life better. There's been many books written about the modern Internet approach to sharing information.

Many companies have become players in their given space by giving things away for free. If nothing else, providing a service and placing their business in a later position for a buyout.

We want to tell a kind story based on human values. When I start working with a company I look for the things they're doing correctly. I look for the ways that they make a positive meaning in people's lives.

Identify the positive things your company is doing for people and I guarantee you have a marketing platform that you can build from. You can create a new story and reinvent the company from there.

What better time than when we reinvent our business to evaluate our strengths? The most powerful strength is to be focused on actually helping people.

CHAPTER *11*

Your Market is World Wide

I made a mention earlier in the book about the opportunities that can happen for you when you realize you are selling to a world audience. It's amazing how many opportunities from all across the globe find you when you tell a consistent marketing story.

This can occur even if you're selling a service. You'd be surprised how many inventive ways can come to you to monetize your services when you are regarded as a worldwide expert.

If nothing else, I've seen people become consultants and start flying all around the world just because people need their opinions.

Yes, We're back to the Importance of Having an Opinion

And to again reinforce one of the earlier points of this book, that's why it is so important that you have an opinion. As I said before, stand for something. If you base your beliefs and market position correctly, others will seek you out.

So you need to expand your world view. Think bigger. Then think bigger again.

No matter what product or service you sell, the odds are very strong that others all around the world can also benefit from your solutions.

This becomes even more true if you develop your unique value proposition correctly. Yep, repeating this again since it is so important!

If you found a way to do something better, you're going to be helping people all around the world by sharing your techniques.

Your Story Earns While You Sleep

One of the greatest things about the Internet is when the light comes on that you can be earning income while you sleep.

I can tell you that personally, I enjoy passive income immensely. I love the idea that valuable contributions I've made continue to work for me 24x7.

Never forget that people in different cultures have the same access by and large to your solutions. Especially if you sell a product that can be ordered online. I'm sure you're very familiar with many success stories of this type.

Nothing is better than generating revenue around the clock. It's one of the secrets that really contributes to a strong market position. It all begins by reinventing your story so customers from around the globe can find your solutions.

Never Say No To A Deal Before Hearing Them Out

Here's an interesting principle. I've spoken with many successful clients who swear by this one. I'm referring to a phenomenon that occurs when someone contacts you independently because they learned about your services and they have an original idea.

I worked with one client who developed a completely new division in another country when somebody contacted them with a turnkey solution. Because my client told a clear marketing story, it was easy for this business person to visualize how my client could easily fit into their marketing. Fit like a glove. And as my client shared, they had learned to never say no to any deal before at least listening and hearing the person out. Very wise counsel.

In this case, it actually was a good deal for my client. An entire new revenue stream, that they never pictured on their own, came to them effortlessly. All because their story made sense.

Start Where You Are

And this all starts by expanding your worldview. Telling a story that can be related to many different diverse cultures. Reinventing yourself and thinking of yourself as a world citizen.

As the tech revolution took off, I began to know more and more people who were traveling to China. We're going to see more traveling and expansion into the world market mindset.

So now it's time for you to get involved. Be sure and expand your world view as you reinvent your story.

CHAPTER 12

Consistent Release Schedules Are Key

As you go about reinventing your business and telling a new story, it's very important that you establish a regular schedule for releasing new information.

There's many different reasons for this. One of the most important reasons is to build your search ranking. Because it's so important, we have been speaking a lot about search engine rankings. I think this is a good use of our time so we'll continue this thread.

I can share my personal experience with clients in this regard. In the instances where my clients have understood how important it is for us to be telling the consistent story on a regular basis, we've been able to achieve spectacular results in our Google profile.

I can't state enough how very important it is to regularly release content. When your story is clearly defined all you need to do is keep releasing stories that are consistent. You can vary themes to keep things interesting, however, you want to keep your overall market story in the forefront.

As I've stated before, no one (outside of Google) knows exactly what algorithms are being used by Google at a given time to determine search ranking.

I can share with you that over many years of experience, I see consistent good results when new content is being released regularly.

This is one of those secrets that's important to understand and adhere to. Google is pretty upfront about this.

Google has repeatedly said that they give precedent to content that actually brings value to a specific niche. In other words, they're going to give more credibility (or ranking) to somebody who sincerely is posting information that's useful.

You can see again how that ties in with everything we've been saying so far in the book. If you're telling a good story, your information is worth publishing. Or placing at the top of the search rankings for the case of our study.

But as I said earlier, you can't fake this. That's why all those tricky search engine techniques fail so badly. They're based on trying to get something for nothing. And they're trying to beat Google at Google's own game. Not wise. Google is much smarter than that.

But for our purposes, we're talking about what really works. And that's where we want to be anyway.

I see this happen all the time. Another reason I recommend you maintain a consistent release schedule is for your own work schedule.

If you know that you need to be releasing new articles every week, you're going to keep working. Steady consistent work over time always makes you an expert on the Internet.

And that is, of course, one of the key objectives of this book.

We want you to be an Internet expert. Ideally, as quick as possible. That's why we want to get you into action. And keep you in action.

I do have some clients that simply don't have the time to do this. For them, it's most expedient and makes a better sense for their marketing mix to have others do the posting of content for them. They hire someone to do this. If that's the case, they still maintain their artistic voice and tone in the communications to ensure that it keeps their marketing story consistent.

I have one client that has created an amazing amount of quality content on the Internet. All organized by metadata and appropriately relevant to their niche. They are at the top of Google search results consistently and are light years ahead of anyone in their field.

When you do a Google search for them entire pages of results are returned! That backs up their earned market position. They are clearly the experts. It's not smoke. Their reputation as leaders in their industry is founded on fact. They've earned their success. They've earned the right to their story.

That's what we want for you!

CHAPTER *13*

Feature Your People

As a producer of commercial video productions, I meet many people in business who turn out to be quite at ease and amazingly persuasive in front of a camera.

Granted, it might not always be the case, but you'd be surprised how many times the very best spokesperson might turn out to be the person who is working right there in your office.

Of course this also extends to the owner themselves. In many cases, no one can tell your story better than you.

I've had the pleasure of working with many owners who came alive in front of the camera. It becomes really easy to see that they genuinely are a caring person. They care about their product or service. And most importantly, they care that you get the quality of services that you deserve.

That's a great story. We've all seen commercials where the founder of the company carries the message better than any spokesperson from Hollywood ever could.

The same can occur when you feature your people. I worked with one client where the nature of their business was dependent on providing ongoing customer services. It was not uncommon for a customer to call the office. We saw that it played well to feature the actual staff who interacted with customers every day on the telephones. They did a great job as the spokespersons in the commercials.

As you can imagine, once we started featuring the staff, their level of dedication increased. A very true marketing maxim... "people support what they create". When you feature your people and give them a chance to shine, they tell your story in an honest way. And what's more, when they're done standing up for your products, they even believe more in your company.

This is especially powerful if you have a type of business that involves one-on-one communications with the customers. As your employees start to believe more in your story, they will tell it with sincerity. Sincerity is the sweet spot.

More About Your Front Line Folks

So many times a business owner is shortsighted

and doesn't realize that the real impression a customer gets of their company occurs the minute someone picks up the phone.

They might be paying that person the least amount in the office and totally clueless to the fact that their telephone staff is setting the entire market impression with the general public.

Many people have had the experience of calling customer support and then finding out the person on the other end doesn't speak English very well. Perhaps this has happened to you. So tell me, what kind of an impression did that make on you? Did it send a message that they care about the quality of their customer service or did it send a message that they're trying to get by as cheaply as possible?

Your people are your story. The highest form of communication is one person to another.

That's why it's so important to feature your folks in the most positive light possible.

I worked with one client where we created an online video FAQ starring the actual office team that answered the phone. This was a great story we were telling. We had customers tell us that they love the fact that they now could put a face together with the voice.

As we analyzed the results of reinventing our

story to include the stars of customer support (thats what they are!), we saw that customers began specifically asking for a person by name.

We also found that customer retention increased. Why? Because we all love community and we love to feel like we belong. These customers said that a specific person had become their friend. The customers now were stakeholders in the business. They cared.

So don't be afraid to give the spotlight to your staff.

People Bring Diverse Skills To TheTable

Another interesting thing that I've observed ties into the fact that it's not uncommon for many of us to have a diverse employment history. In other words, I've seen people who had a history of public speaking contribute amazingly once they're put in front of the camera.

They were sleepers. Nobody knew they had that kind of experience or talents.

A woman working in the office had been a newscaster. Once we put her in front of the microphone she was amazing. Customers loved her.

Feature your people. You'll be glad you did.

CHAPTER 14

Outsourcing Your Web Programming and The Importance of Your Story

Extensive changes have occurred due to changing economic conditions. Many companies now outsource many of their web development functions.

Because of these changes, I would like to address the importance of having your marketing story administered correctly.

There are, of course, many derivations of outsourcing models involved in the web development environment for a company. Let's examine a few of the common scenarios.

One scenario that has been embraced and adopted by many companies in the United States is outsourcing to a programmer or team of programmers in another country. While it does save them overhead by not having to pay direct salaries, health insurance, or other traditional overhead costs there are however some important considerations.

Many times programmers in another country do not understand the culture nor do they understand how to convey a company story. I've actually run into this a number of different times. Although the programmers from another country are technically proficient, the consistency and integrity of the company story is lost as they take over web tasks.

A Solution for Offshore Outsourcing

I've been called in as a consultant for several of these operations that involve offshore outsourcing. Our solution has been to set up a web team in the United States to oversee the client's story. The purpose is to make sure that all communications maintain the unique perspective that is critical for the continuance of the clients market positions and for ongoing solutions for the customers.

A small crew can effectively act as an editorial team and ensure that every detail maintains the integrity of their story. When technological and programming projects are required, the offshore personnel can continue to provide the programming tasks at reduced pricing structure.

This allows the United States employer to still save money. Their on site editorial team provides focus to ensure the marketing story makes sense to customers.

CHAPTER 15

Telling Your Story Using Temp Workers

Another scenario that we're seeing more often involves using temp workers through employment agencies in the United States.

In this scenario, the company makes a decision to outsource their web development to a temp agency that will subsequently assign workers as needed.

In speaking to the human resource teams of many of these companies, they've been quite clear. Due to changing economic conditions, many of them have simply had to make the decision to lay off their usual web team and to use temp workers for basic maintenance and occasional development operations.

As consultants we found that a similar solution to outsourcing often provides benefits for these companies.

This again involves the creation of editorial web teams. The main function of these teams is to collate, organize, and administer all of the content messaging in the company's marketing mix.

While it certainly might be a preferable scenario to maintain an entire on staff team, we have found that the message and the story can maintain integrity when an editorial web team administers the content message.

CHAPTER *16*

If It's Fun For You, It's Probably Fun For Them

It's been quoted quite often but it's worth saying again. The late great Joseph Campbell was credited with the following slogan… "Follow your bliss!"

Not only was this good advice as he counseled the young students at Sarah Lawrence University, it's good advice for all of us today.

As we've been discussing the various principles in telling your story, I hope it's become clear how important it is to… well, have fun.

This falls right into line too with living a story of integrity. I can tell you, I only work with clients that I enjoy being around. Life is too short.

Plus, people respond to joy. I truly enjoy myself when I can consult with a client and point out positive things about them. People light up. For good reason.

Everyone deserves to be seen in the best light possible.

The world keeps changing and ideally your story includes enjoying your business. The more fun you have, the better the odds you'll remain in your integrity.

Make a Difference

When you successfully reinvent your business, it's my hope that you'll also increase your enthusiasm as you develop your awareness. You can make a difference.

The client who really gets this starts to enjoy their business more than they ever did before.

It makes you feel great to realize that your story reaches people and makes their life better. It makes you willing to work harder when you realize your efforts are rewarded in returns.

That's the kind of thing that happens when you tell a new story and reinvent your business.

As I mentioned earlier, we can pretty much count on the fact that technology is going to keep changing. The democratization of tools means that many people can now access tools that used to be held by just a few select professionals.

The powerful explosion of online video is a

great example. New cameras, editing suites, even special effects are in the hands of more people today than at any time in history. This is an exciting time to be a storyteller!

And that's exactly what I'm attempting to do with you… turn you into a world-class storyteller!

I understand that we've been focusing a lot on values, attitudes, and principles.

I'm not trying to be a cheerleader. I do believe that when we tell a positive story, we get a positive outcome. And at the end of the day, that's time well spent.

I hope you agree. For when these bedrock principles are in place, no matter how the world changes, you will always have your place. You'll always fit in.

And to the degree that you develop your ability to tell stories, there will be other benefits also.

For one thing, you will become much more efficient in meetings. As many of you know, there is nothing worse than a meandering meeting that goes nowhere.

As you become an efficient storyteller, you learn to get to the point.

You also get to where you understand what is

your story's singular key point. When you know your key point, you understand what you really need to communicate. From there, they either want what you have to offer or they don't. That saves you from a lot of useless waste of time.

You know your story. You know how to tell your story. That's all you need.

Thanks so much for hanging in there with me throughout this book. I look forward to having the opportunity to meet you.

In the following pages I've listed my contact information. I love helping folks and talking about the art of creating successful business stories, so please feel free to get in touch.

Epilogue

I want to thank you again for spending time with
me in this book.

I look forward to speaking with you.
Please feel free to get in touch.

MEDIA1250 CONSULTING
WWW.MEDIA1250.COM

MARK ORION
MEDIA1250@GMAIL.COM
AUSTIN, TEXAS
(512) 422-9966

ABOUT THE AUTHOR

MARK ORION has advised top Fortune 500 companies on Internet and Web projects and is recognized as a leading authority on Website technologies and the development of strategic marketing initiatives for the Internet.

He has addressed thousands as an industry spokesman at Web conferences and directed Web task forces and project teams for clients that include Dell, Microsoft, Apple, IBM, and PBS TV.

In addition to recognized programming and computer skills, his expertise extends to film, video, and television productions.

He currently resides in the Austin, Texas area.

The 10 Minutes With a Professional Series

These books are a series of expert manuals.

Designed to quickly share an author's area of expertise,
the **10 Minutes With a Professional Series** features
select authors speaking on a diverse set of subject matter.